See the Stars

YOUR FIRST GUIDE TO THE NIGHT SKY

KEN CROSWELL

Boyds Mills Press

ACKNOWLEDGMENTS

I thank Akira Fujii for allowing me to use his beautiful constellation photographs as well as his photograph of the Double Cluster. For the other photographs in this book, I thank the Anglo-Australian Observatory, Kitt Peak National Observatory, NASA, and Mike Sisk.

I thank Terence Dickinson, Alan MacRobert, and Fred Schaaf for reading the manuscript and offering their comments.

For their support of this project, I thank my agent, Lew Grimes; my editor, Andy Boyles; and my publisher, Kent L. Brown Jr.

Photo credits:
All constellation photographs copyright © Akira Fujii.
Orion Nebula, page 7, copyright © Mike Sisk.
Lagoon Nebula, page 21, copyright © Association of Universities for Research in Astronomy (AURA).
National Optical Astronomy Observatories (NOAO)/National Science Foundation (NSF).
Double Cluster, page 25, copyright © Akira Fujii.
Pleiades, page 29, copyright © Anglo-Australian Observatory/Royal Observatory Edinburgh (photo made from UK Schmidt plates by David Malin).
Venus, page 30, NASA/Pioneer Venus. Courtesy National Space Science Data Center (NSSDC).
Mars, page 30, NASA/Viking/U.S. Geological Survey. Courtesy NSSDC.
Jupiter, page 30, NASA/Voyager 1. Courtesy NSSDC.
Saturn, page 30, NASA/Voyager 2. Courtesy NSSDC.

Published by Caroline House
Boyds Mills Press, Inc.
A Highlights Company
815 Church Street
Honesdale, Pennsylvania 18431
Printed in China

U.S. Cataloging-in-Publication Data
  (Library of Congress Standards)

Croswell, Ken.
    See the Stars : your first guide to the night sky / by Ken Croswell.
—1st ed.
[32] p. : col. Ill. ; cm.
Includes index.
Summary: A book of twelve star-gazing activities, one for each month of the year.
ISBN 1-56397-757-5
1. Stars. 2. Astronomy. 3. Cosmology. I. Title.
523—dc21   2000   AC CIP
99-68078

First edition, 2000
Book designed by Jeff George
The text of this book is set in 11-point New Century Schoolbook.

10 9 8 7 6 5 4

Visit our Web site:
www.boydsmillspress.com

Orion Nebula

A Galaxy of Stars

Stars, stars, stars—red, blue, yellow, orange, white. So many stars! Thousands shine tonight, twinkling after sunset. Stars make patterns, called constellations, that look like dippers, kites, teapots, and even people. This book will help you learn the most important constellations and their stars.

A star is a hot ball of gas that gives off light in the darkness of space. You already know one star—the Sun—but you may not think of it that way. The Sun looks different from other stars because it is much closer to us. That's because we live on Earth, a planet that goes around the Sun. If we lived on another planet going around another star, that star would look much like the Sun, and the Sun would be just another star in the night. So when you look at a star, you may be looking at someone else's sun.

Without stars, life would not exist. The Sun warms the Earth, and its light makes plants grow, giving us food. Plus, before the Sun and Earth were born, other stars created most of the chemical elements—such as carbon, oxygen, calcium, and iron—that now make up our world, and our bodies.

Stars live in galaxies. Every star you can see without using binoculars or a telescope belongs to our Galaxy, the Milky Way. Altogether, the Milky Way Galaxy contains more than 100,000,000,000 stars. So the Milky Way has more stars than the Earth has people. And beyond the Milky Way are billions of other galaxies, each with its own stars.

If the sky is clear, you can see the stars *tonight*—and you don't need a telescope. But where do you begin? There are so many stars up there, and at first they all look the same.

Well, that's the reason for this book. Each month, you can explore a new constellation. You'll see places where new stars are being born, clusters brimming with hundreds of young stars, old stars that are about to die, and even regions containing black holes. Along the way, you'll see two dippers, a lion, a shepherd, a harp, a swan, a scorpion, a queen, and a bull.

Ready? Just turn the page. . . .

How to Use This Book

To find the constellations in this book, just follow these easy steps.

1. Figure out which way is north, east, south, and west. You can look at a map that shows which direction your street runs. Or you can use the Sun, which rises in one direction and sets in another.

Month	Sunrise	Sunset
January	Southeast	Southwest
February	East	West
March	East	West
April	East	West
May	Northeast	Northwest
June	Northeast	Northwest
July	Northeast	Northwest
August	East	West
September	East	West
October	East	West
November	Southeast	Southwest
December	Southeast	Southwest

For example, in March, the Sun sets in the west. So when you face the setting Sun, west is in front of you, east is behind you, north is on your right, and south is on your left.

2. Gather what you'll need. You *don't* need a telescope, but you might want binoculars, to help you see the stars better. You should also have a flashlight, so you'll be able to read in the dark. It's best if the flashlight emits dim red light, because red light does not ruin your ability to see in the dark as much as white light does. If you don't have a red flashlight, you can put a piece of red plastic or a few pieces of red cellophane over the front of a white flashlight.

3. Turn to the page that matches the current month. Before you go outside, read about what you'll be exploring. Look at the diagram and find the same pattern of stars in the photograph. Now look at the table inside the yellow box to see when and where to look.

4. Dress warmly. You won't be moving around much, so you'll really feel the cold. A good rule to follow: dress as though it were 20 degrees Fahrenheit (10 degrees Celsius) colder than it really is. For example, if it's 50 degrees Fahrenheit (10 degrees Celsius), dress as though it were 30 degrees Fahrenheit (about 0 degrees Celsius).

5. Go outside at the right time and find a dark place, away from any lights, if possible. Then you'll be able to see the stars better, especially the faint ones. Be sure you're in a safe place—you may want someone to go with you. Also, it's best if the Moon is not out, since its glare washes out faint stars.

6. Look in the direction given for the date and time in the yellow box.

7. Now try to match the bright stars in the photograph with the bright stars in that part of the sky. If the photograph has the label, "Turn photograph so that this edge faces north," then you may have to tilt the photograph. For example, if you are facing east, then north will be on your left. Turn the book so that the north part of the photograph is on your left.

The photograph shows many more stars than you can see. Pay attention only to the bright stars in the photograph and try to find the same pattern of stars shown in the diagram. Be patient. It takes several minutes for your eyes to adjust to the dark, and it may take even longer to find what you're looking for. Sometimes you may think that you have the right star, then discover that you don't. If that happens, just try another star. If you still don't succeed, make sure that you're looking in the right direction and at the right time.

8. After you've found the constellation and enjoyed its sights, you may want to see more stars. Usually, the constellations from the month before and the month after are also visible—check the yellow boxes throughout the book. For example, if it's December, you can see that month's featured constellation, plus the ones from November and January.

This book works best if you live between latitudes 30 and 50 degrees north. This zone includes most of the United States, southern Canada, Japan, Korea, China north of Shanghai, Israel, and the southern half of Europe. If you live somewhat north of this zone—for example, in Alaska, England, northern Germany, or Poland— you can still use this book, but you will have trouble seeing two southern constellations, Scorpius and Sagittarius. If you live somewhat south of this zone—for example, in Florida, Hawaii, or southern China—then you can also use this book, but there will be times when you won't be able to see the Big Dipper and Cassiopeia.

Winter nights bring the most glorious constellation: Orion the Hunter, which shines over snowy fields and icy streets. Orion abounds with bright stars, including a red one and a blue one. It even has a place where new stars are being born.

Check the yellow box to see when and where to look for Orion tonight. Then look for a pattern of bright stars that matches the pattern in the photograph. A special part of the pattern is made by three stars lined up beside one another. This is Orion's belt. Above and to the left of the belt is an even brighter star, Betelgeuse, which marks one of Orion's shoulders; below and to the right of the belt is another bright star, Rigel, one of his legs.

Even though the stars in Orion appear together, they actually are at different distances from us. Betelgeuse is about 430 light-years away, while Rigel is about 800 light-years away. That means the light you see from Betelgeuse started out 430 years ago, but the light from Rigel started out 800 years ago—long before Christopher Columbus sailed the Atlantic Ocean.

These stars are different colors. Can you see that Betelgeuse is reddish and Rigel is bluish? If not, stare at Rigel for half a minute and then look at Betelgeuse. Betelgeuse should look fiery red. If you still have trouble seeing the color difference, try looking at the stars through binoculars. Betelgeuse is the only bright star in Orion that is red. The others are blue, like Rigel.

Stars are different colors because they have different temperatures. When metal is heated, it first glows red. As it gets hotter, the metal turns orange, then yellow, then white, then blue-white. The same is true with stars. All stars are hot, but some are hotter than others. Blue stars like Rigel are hotter than red ones like Betelgeuse. The yellow Sun is in between.

After you've checked out Rigel and Betelgeuse, take a look at the three stars lined up in the middle of Orion, Orion's belt. All three are hot and blue.

Orion's belt can lead you to stars in other constellations. Draw a line from lower left to upper right through the three stars and continue on for quite a way. You'll come to Aldebaran, an orange star in Taurus (DECEMBER). Draw a line through the belt in the opposite direction and you'll reach Sirius, the brightest star in the night. Sirius is a white star just about 8½ light-years away, much closer than the stars of Orion.

Below Orion's belt is a column of fainter stars that make up his sword. With binoculars, you can see that one of the "stars" in the sword looks fuzzy.

That "star" is really a cloud of gas and dust called a nebula. The Orion Nebula is giving birth to new stars.

All stars were born in places like the Orion Nebula. So was the Sun, 4½ billion years ago. Someday, the stars forming in the Orion Nebula may have planets like Earth going around them.

Where and When to Look

On these dates	Look	Around this time
December 1 to 15	Southeast	10 p.m.
December 16 to 31	Southeast	9 p.m.
January 1 to 15	Southeast	8 p.m.
January 16 to 31	South	9 p.m.
February 1 to 14	South	8 p.m.
February 15 to 28	South	7 p.m.
March 1 to 15	Southwest	8 p.m.
March 16 to 31	Southwest	7 p.m.
April 1 to 15	West	9 p.m.

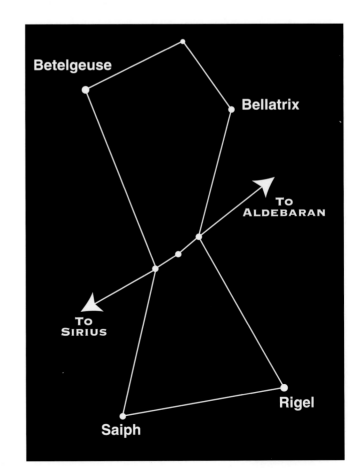

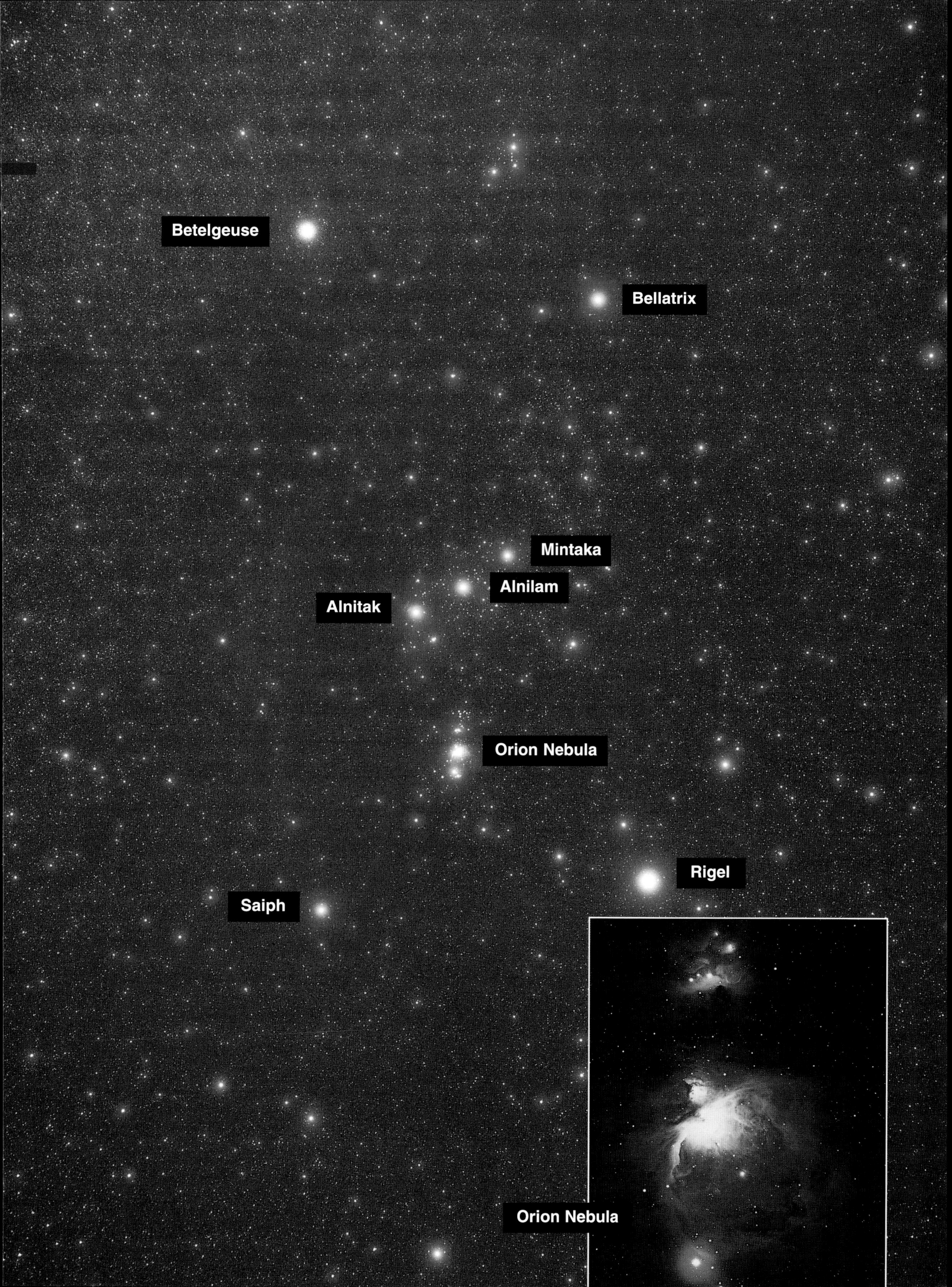

Betelgeuse

Bellatrix

Mintaka

Alnilam

Alnitak

Orion Nebula

Rigel

Saiph

Orion Nebula

The Big Dipper is a famous star pattern. You can use it to find other stars, including the North Star.

Look for the Big Dipper at the time and place given in the yellow box. If the Big Dipper is in the northeast, its bowl will be higher than its handle—turn the photograph so that the star labels are right-side up. If the Big Dipper is in the northwest, its handle will be higher than its bowl—turn the photograph so that the star labels are upside down. Sometimes people complain that constellations don't look like what they're supposed to. You can't say that about the Big Dipper! It really looks like a dipper—and it's BIG, much bigger than it looks in the photograph.

The Big Dipper has seven stars. The four stars in the bowl are Dubhe, Merak, Phecda, and Megrez. The three stars in the handle are Alioth, Mizar, and Alkaid. Can you see that Megrez—the star that joins the bowl to the handle—is fainter than the other six?

The five middle stars, from Merak to Mizar, are all about 80 light-years from Earth. They travel through space together, so they were probably born together.

Using binoculars, look at Mizar, the star next to the handle's end. You will see two stars. The fainter is named Alcor. Together, Mizar and Alcor form a double star, sometimes called the Horse and Rider. Mizar is the horse. Alcor is the rider.

Now let the Big Dipper lead you to a star in another constellation. Imagine a line from Merak to Dubhe—two of the bowl stars—and follow the line onward. You will come to a star as bright as they are. This is the famous North Star, also known as Polaris. When you look at Polaris, you are facing due north. So now you can tell exactly where north is.

Polaris is always there. It is the only star that appears to stay in one place, all night and all year. Other stars, including the Sun, seem to move. For example, after an hour, stars in the east will be higher in the sky and stars in the west will be lower.

To understand why Polaris doesn't move, stand in a room beneath a lightbulb. If you spin around, the walls and windows appear to swing around you, even though they are not really moving. In the same way, stars don't really move across the sky—they only seem to, because the Earth spins. While you are turning, you'll see that the lightbulb above you does *not* move. Likewise, 430 light-years away, Polaris is right above Earth's north pole, so it always appears to be in the same place.

Polaris is in a dipper of its own, the Little Dipper, which also has seven stars. Polaris is at the end of the Little Dipper's handle. But the Little Dipper is harder to see, because most of its stars are fainter. You might see only two or three of them.

The Big Dipper can lead you to still more stars. If you use the other two stars in the bowl—Megrez and Phecda—and follow them *away* from the North Star, you will come to Regulus, the brightest star in Leo (MARCH). And if you follow the curve of the handle away from the bowl, you will reach beautiful Arcturus in Boötes (APRIL).

Where and When to Look

On these dates	Look	Around this time
January	Northeast	8 p.m.
February	Northeast	8 p.m.
March	Northeast	8 p.m.
April	Overhead	9 p.m.
May	Overhead	10 p.m.
June	Northwest	10 p.m.
July	Northwest	10 p.m.
August	Northwest	10 p.m.
September	Northwest	9 p.m.
October	Northwest	8 p.m.
November	Low North	8 p.m.
December	Low North	8 p.m.

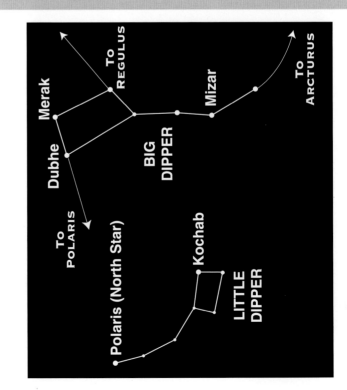

March LEO THE LION

During the windy weather of March, a constellation rises whose mighty roar matches the month itself: Leo the Lion. Unlike many constellations, Leo really looks like what it's supposed to.

As befits the king of the animals, Leo is big. The bright star Regulus marks Leo's heart. North of Regulus is a sickle of stars that looks like a backward question mark. This is his head and mane. The faint star in front of Regulus, Omicron Leonis, marks his forepaws, which stretch out in front of him. Far to the other side of Regulus is a triangle of stars—his rear and tail. The last star is Denebola, whose name means "tail of the lion."

You can find Leo at the time and place listed in the yellow box. If Leo is in the east, his head will be higher than his tail. He will look like he's leaping up from the horizon. If Leo is in the west, his head will be lower than his tail.

The name of Leo's brightest star, Regulus, means "little king." The light you are seeing actually left Regulus 77 years ago. Regulus is a blue star that is hotter and brighter than the Sun. If you gaze at Regulus through binoculars, you will see its color better.

Other stars you might want to look at are Algeiba, a beautiful yellow star in Leo's mane, and Denebola, the tail star, which is white.

Leo is famous not just for its stars but also because it belongs to the zodiac. The zodiac is the zone where the Sun, the Moon, and the planets appear. So if you see a bright "star" in Leo that's not in the photograph, it is probably a planet. That's the reason for the PLANET ALERT! Once a month, the Moon moves through Leo, so you might see the Moon here, too.

The zodiac forms a belt around the sky because the Sun, the Moon, and the planets are close to being on a single plane. To picture this, imagine running around a track with other runners. You see lots of runners, but they are not everywhere you look. You see them in front of you, in back of you, to your left, and to your right, but you don't see any above or below you. In the same way, our planet, the Earth, is racing around the Sun. So are the Sun's other planets. When we look "up" (north) or "down" (south), we see no planets. But when we look to one side or the other, at a zodiac constellation like Leo, we may see a planet or two.

Where and When to Look

On these dates		Look	Around this time
February	1 to 14	East	10 p.m.
February	15 to 28	East	9 p.m.
March		East	8 p.m.
April	1 to 15	High East	9 p.m.
April	16 to 30	Overhead	9 p.m.
May	1 to 15	Overhead	9 p.m.
May	16 to 31	West	10 p.m.
June		West	10 p.m.

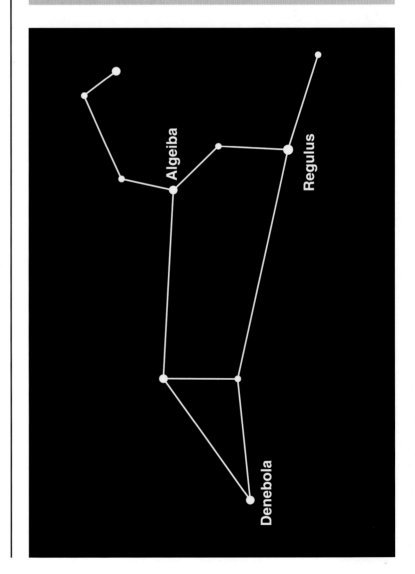

Omicron
Leonis

Regulus

Algeiba

Denebola

Planet Alert!

If you see a bright "star" in this constellation which is not on the photograph, it is probably a planet! See page 30 to figure out which one.

April
BOÖTES THE HERDSMAN

Every spring, after the cold winter, I look forward to the arrival of beautiful Arcturus, the brightest star in Boötes. Arcturus is a brilliant orange gem that signals warmer weather ahead. It also foretells the future of our Sun.

Boötes is supposed to look like a herdsman, but if you can see a herdsman here, you are a better astronomer than I am. To me, Boötes looks like a kite. Other people see it as an ice-cream cone.

To find Boötes, first find Arcturus. There are two ways to do it. You can look in the direction given in the yellow box and search for a bright orange star. But there's another way I like better. You must first find the Big Dipper (FEBRUARY). Follow the curve of the Big Dipper's handle away from the bowl for one Dipper length and you'll come to Arcturus. If you follow the curve beyond Arcturus, you'll reach another bright star, Spica. It shines in the constellation Virgo. Spica is blue.

Once you've found Arcturus, try to find the five other stars that make up the pattern of Boötes. They are north of Arcturus. They are harder to see, since they are fainter.

Of all the stars in the sky, Arcturus is my favorite, because of its brilliance and beautiful orange color. Of the nighttime stars I can see, only the winter star Sirius (JANUARY) shines brighter. But Sirius is white, whereas Arcturus sparkles orange. Gaze at it through binoculars and watch it flicker like a far-off fire. The orange color means that Arcturus is somewhat cooler than the Sun, which is yellow. You might compare Arcturus with blue Spica, whose color indicates it is hotter than the Sun.

Arcturus's name means "bear keeper," because it is close to the Big and Little Dippers. The Big Dipper is part of Ursa Major, the Great Bear, and the Little Dipper is also called Ursa Minor, the Little Bear. So Arcturus watches over the two bears.

As stars go, Arcturus is nearby, just 37 light-years from Earth. So the light you see tonight left Arcturus 37 years ago.

Arcturus is different from the Sun, for it is a giant, a star that is bigger and brighter than the Sun. It sends out more than a hundred times more light. A billion years ago, though, Arcturus was a yellow star that resembled the Sun. The Sun shines because nuclear reactions at its center turn hydrogen into helium and make energy. But Arcturus's center ran out of hydrogen, so the star began burning hydrogen outside its center. This new energy source caused the star to expand, brighten, and cool, and it turned from yellow to orange.

Someday, the same thing will happen to the Sun—but not for billions of years, so we don't have to worry about it. For now, Arcturus is a wonderful sight, and a promise that its color will soon be mirrored in countless flowers blooming this spring.

Where and When to Look

On these dates		Look	Around this time
March	1 to 15	Northeast	10 p.m.
March	16 to 31	Northeast	9 p.m.
April	1 to 15	East	10 p.m.
April	16 to 30	East	9 p.m.
May	1 to 15	High East	9 p.m.
May	16 to 31	Overhead	10 p.m.
June		Overhead	10 p.m.
July		High West	10 p.m.
August	1 to 15	West	10 p.m.
August	16 to 31	West	9 p.m.
September	1 to 15	Northwest	9 p.m.
September	16 to 30	Northwest	8 p.m.

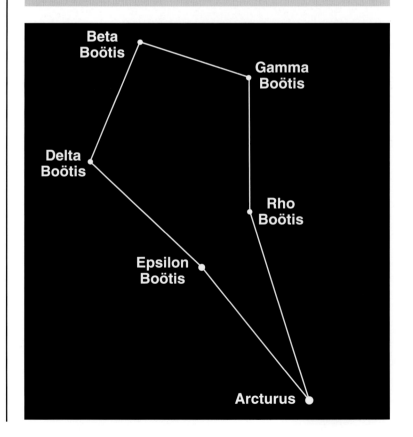

TURN PHOTOGRAPH SO THAT THIS EDGE FACES NORTH.

Beta Boötis

Gamma Boötis

Delta Boötis

Rho Boötis

Epsilon Boötis

Arcturus

May LYRA THE LYRE

Lyra the Lyre, a harplike instrument, is unique. It is the only musical instrument in the sky.

To locate Lyra, look in the direction listed in the yellow box for the brightest white star. That's Vega. The rest of the constellation is much fainter, and it's very small. If you stretch out your arm, Lyra will be about as short as your thumb. Look first for the two stars that make a tiny triangle with Vega: Epsilon and Zeta Lyrae. Then look for the parallelogram of Delta, Zeta, Beta, and Gamma Lyrae. Beta and Gamma Lyrae are easier to see than the other two.

Lyra's lead star, Vega, is beautiful. It's just 25 light-years from Earth. Look at it through binoculars, and you'll see a brilliant white light tinged with sparks of blue. Vega was the first nighttime star ever photographed, in 1850.

To the Chinese, Vega was a princess, in love with a herdsman who is represented by another bright star, Altair, in the constellation Aquila. You can find Altair by drawing a line from Vega through Gamma Lyrae and continuing far on until you come to a bright star. According to the story, Vega and Altair spent so much time together that they neglected their duties. So Vega's father separated them by putting them on opposite sides of the Milky Way, which the Chinese saw as a great river. But a tearful Vega extracted this promise from her father: on one night of every year—the seventh night of the seventh moon—a bridge of birds will span the river's waters and allow the two lovers an evening together.

The Sun is a single star, but many stars are double, triple, or quadruple. Next to Vega in Lyra is the famous "double-double" star, Epsilon Lyrae. Look at it through binoculars and you'll see two stars. A few people—not me!—can see that Epsilon Lyrae is double even without binoculars. Can you? If you had a telescope, each of the two stars would also look double, which is why it's called the "double-double" star. So altogether, Epsilon Lyrae has four stars. They are all 160 light-years from Earth.

If you like Epsilon Lyrae, look at Zeta Lyrae (the star that joins the triangle to the parallelogram) and Delta Lyrae (next to Zeta). Both are double, too. Delta Lyrae is especially beautiful, because the two stars are red and blue.

Lyra holds yet another double star for you to see—but in a different way. It is Beta Lyrae, one of the stars at the base of the parallelogram. It won't look double through binoculars. But every 13 days, the fainter of the two stars moves in front of the brighter one and blocks its light, so Beta Lyrae fades. Normally, Beta Lyrae looks as bright as Gamma Lyrae, the other star in the base of the parallelogram. But during an eclipse, it fades and looks much fainter. As you might guess, a star whose light varies is called a variable star. Check out Beta Lyrae tonight. Is it as bright as Gamma Lyrae? Or have you caught it in eclipse?

Where and When to Look

On these dates		Look	Around this time
May		Northeast	10 p.m.
June		East	10 p.m.
July	1 to 15	High East	10 p.m.
July	16 to 31	Overhead	10 p.m.
August	1 to 15	Overhead	10 p.m.
August	16 to 31	Overhead	9 p.m.
September	1 to 15	Overhead	9 p.m.
September	16 to 30	Overhead	8 p.m.
October		High West	8 p.m.
November		West	7 p.m.
December		Northwest	7 p.m.

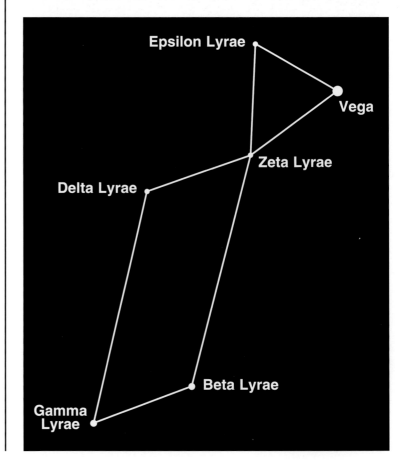

TURN PHOTOGRAPH SO THAT THIS EDGE FACES NORTH.

Epsilon Lyrae

Vega

Zeta Lyrae

Delta Lyrae

Beta Lyrae

Gamma Lyrae

June CYGNUS THE SWAN

Tonight you can see a constellation that harbors two black holes: Cygnus the Swan, which resembles a gigantic cross.

Look at Cygnus in the photograph and in the diagram. Cygnus's brightest star, Deneb, is the Swan's tail; Deneb means "tail." Albireo, a fainter star, is the Swan's head, and the span from Epsilon to Delta Cygni represents the Swan's wings. However, I see Cygnus as a cross, with Deneb at the top. People often call Cygnus the Northern Cross.

To find Cygnus, look in the direction given in the yellow box. Search for a bright star—Deneb. It is easy to see, but it won't be as bright as some of the other stars in the sky. If you've got the right star, then to its south you should see the five other stars that make up a large cross.

Deneb is a white star that doesn't look that impressive. But it *is* impressive, because it shines from a distance of some 1,800 light-years—farther away than any other bright star. In order to look so bright from so far, Deneb must be powerful. It pours out more light in a single night than the Sun does in an entire century. Sometimes what you know is more impressive than what you see.

Black holes are another example. A black hole is a star that you can't see. Its gravity is so great that not even light—the fastest thing in the universe—can escape. Since it emits no light, it is black. And because once you fall in you can't get out, it's a hole. That's why astronomers call it a black hole.

The most famous black hole is Cygnus X-1. It was once a bright star like Deneb. But it ran out of fuel and collapsed under its own weight, pressing itself into a tiny point. To find this black hole, look at Eta Cygni, the star in the long, bottom section of the cross. When you look at Eta Cygni, you will also be looking in the direction of Cygnus X-1, which is just east of Eta Cygni but thousands of light-years beyond. Of course, you won't see the black hole itself, but now you know where it is. And if you like black holes, there's another one midway between Eta Cygni and Epsilon Cygni (in the wing), V404 Cygni.

Right now you may be asking: if we can't see black holes, how do we know they're there? In each case, a visible star goes around a massive object that no one can see, and astronomers deduce that the dark star is a black hole.

For something that you *can* see, look at Albireo, the star at the bottom of the cross. Albireo is a beautiful double star, with one star orange and the other one blue. If your binoculars are good, and if you hold them rock steady by propping them up

against a tree or a fence, you'll see the two stars very close together.

If you can't, don't despair. Another double star looks a lot like it: 31 Cygni, whose two stars are also orange and blue. It's easier to see 31 Cygni's stars separately. This double star is near Deneb, toward Delta Cygni, and is a lovely sight through binoculars.

Where and When to Look

On these dates		Look	Around this time
June		Northeast	10 p.m.
July		East	10 p.m.
August	1 to 15	Overhead	10 p.m.
August	16 to 31	Overhead	9 p.m.
September	1 to 15	Overhead	9 p.m.
September	16 to 30	Overhead	8 p.m.
October		Overhead	8 p.m.
November		West	8 p.m.
December		West	7 p.m.

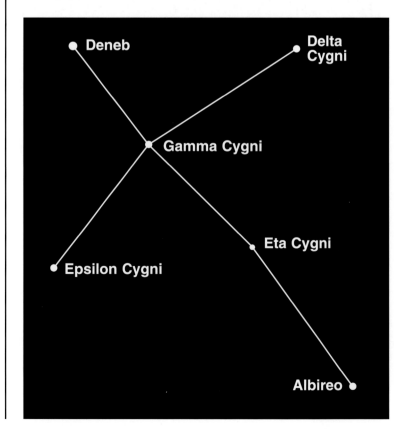

16

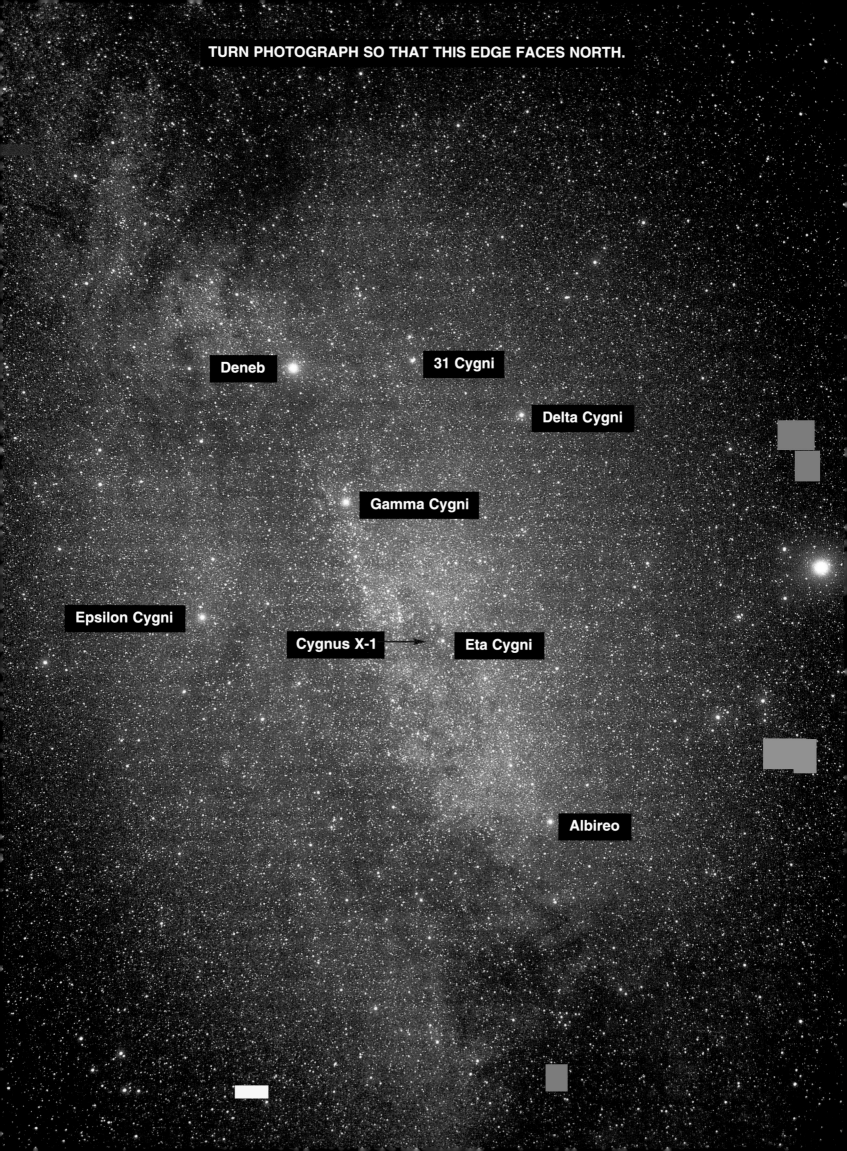

July
SCORPIUS THE SCORPION

Summer nights feature a constellation representing a creature that is both deadly and beautiful. Scorpius the Scorpion is bright, complete with a stunning red star. But there's a catch. Scorpius is far to the south, so it never rises high nor stays around long.

During winter, you may have seen brilliant Orion the Hunter (JANUARY). Well, don't look for him now. According to one story, Orion boasted so much about killing animals that Scorpius was sent to get even by stinging him. So when Scorpius rises, Orion sets, which means you won't see both at once.

To locate Scorpius, find a clear view to the south. Then look for a bright red star, Antares, which marks Scorpius's heart. On each side of Antares is a fainter star, one below and to the left (Tau Scorpii), the other above and to the right (Sigma Scorpii). Once you've found Antares and its two companions, look farther right for three stars in a crooked up-and-down line—Scorpius's head.

On the other side of Antares is Scorpius's tail, which starts with Epsilon Scorpii. The name of the bright star near the tail's end, Shaula, means "the sting." No wonder Orion sets when Scorpius rises!

Tracing out the tail might be tough, since some stars may be below the horizon. If you can't find them all, don't worry; there are plenty of sights near Antares, starting with Antares itself. Take a look at the star through binoculars. It is a beautiful red. Its name means "rival of Mars," because it looks like the red planet. The Chinese called it the Fire Star. Antares is 600 light-years from Earth. It is an enormous star called a red supergiant. If the Sun were that big, it would swallow Mercury, Venus, Earth, and Mars.

If the sky is dark, you may detect through binoculars a dim, fuzzy glow to the right of Antares. This is a star cluster that houses hundreds of thousands of stars. Named M4, it is more than ten times farther away than Antares.

Unlike Antares, most bright stars in Scorpius are blue—like the two on either side of Antares, the three in Scorpius's head, and Shaula near the tail's end. These blue stars, plus red Antares, belong to the Scorpius-Centaurus Association, a group that was born together and moves through space together.

In the tail of Scorpius, you can see a double blue star, Mu Scorpii. Look at this star through binoculars. Its two stars both belong to the Scorpius-Centaurus Association. One legend says they are two children fleeing evil parents.

Once you've found Scorpius, it's easy to find another constellation: Sagittarius (AUGUST), which is to the left of Scorpius.

Where and When to Look

On these dates		Look	Around this time
July	1 to 15	South	11 p.m.
July	16 to 31	South	10 p.m.
August	1 to 15	Southwest	10 p.m.
August	16 to 31	Southwest	9 p.m.

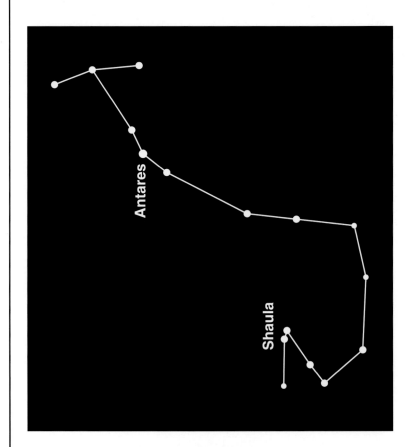

Planet Alert!
If you see a bright "star" in this constellation which is not on the photograph, it is probably a planet! See page 30 to figure out which one.

18

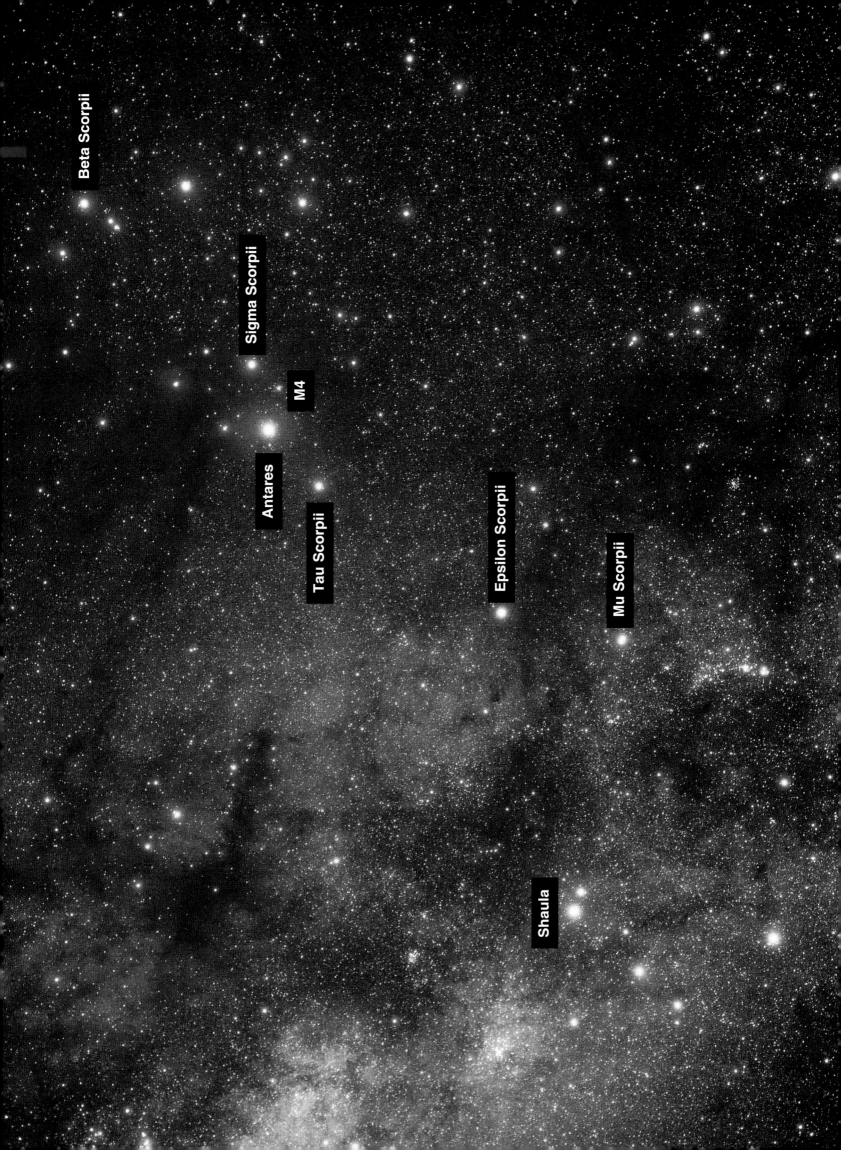

August SAGITTARIUS THE ARCHER

Sagittarius decorates the southern sky on summer nights. It lacks spectacular stars, but it makes a neat pattern that resembles something you might find in your kitchen. Sagittarius is also special because it houses the center of our Galaxy.

Sagittarius is supposed to be an archer, shooting an arrow at Scorpius, the deadly scorpion to his right. Well, I'm sorry, but Sagittarius doesn't look like that at all. Instead, its eight main stars make the shape of a teapot. The three stars on the right are the spout, the four stars on the left make the handle, and the star at the top crowns the lid.

To find the teapot in the sky, go to a place with a clear view to the south. If you already know where Scorpius is, just look to the left of it. If not, look in the direction given in the yellow box. Remember that the stars aren't super bright, and look for a teapot. Nice, isn't it?

The eight stars of the teapot are between 77 and 310 light-years from Earth. You can look at them through binoculars. Far beyond, at a distance of 27,000 light-years, is the heart of our Galaxy, the Milky Way. The Milky Way's brightest stars, including the Sun, nestle in a disk that resembles a pancake—but this pancake is 120,000 light-years across and 2,000 light-years thick.

You probably know that the Moon goes around the Earth and the Earth goes around the Sun. But did you know that the Sun goes around the center of the Galaxy? Every hour, the Sun and Earth race half a million miles through space. But our Galaxy is so big that even at such speed, the Sun takes 230 million years to go around the Galaxy once. In contrast, the Earth goes around the Sun in just a year, and the Moon goes around the Earth in about a month. Every other star you see also goes around the Milky Way's center.

The Galactic center is just above and to the right of the teapot's spout. You won't be able to see the actual center, because gas and dust block the light of the stars there. The very center emits no light anyway, because it is a giant black hole. A black hole swallows everything that falls into it, even light. But we don't have to worry about being sucked into it, since it's so far away.

As the home of the Milky Way's center, Sagittarius hosts many sights, such as stars and star clusters, plus clouds of gas and dust. These gas clouds look like tiny patches of smoke, and you can see them by sweeping over the constellation with binoculars. Take a look at the Lagoon Nebula, above the teapot's spout. It's a cloud of gas and dust that's giving birth to new stars.

If you haven't yet seen Scorpius (JULY), this might be a good time to try; it's to the right of Sagittarius and bears a beautiful red star.

Where and When to Look

On these dates		Look	Around this time
July	15 to 31	Southeast	10 p.m.
August	1 to 15	South	10 p.m.
August	16 to 31	South	9 p.m.
September 1 to 15		Southwest	10 p.m.
September 16 to 30		Southwest	9 p.m.
October	1 to 15	Southwest	8 p.m.
October	16 to 31	Southwest	7 p.m.

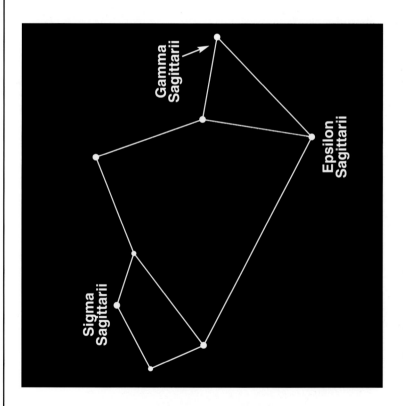

Gamma Sagittarii

Epsilon Sagittarii

Sigma Sagittarii

Planet Alert!
If you see a bright "star" in this constellation which is not on the photograph, it is probably a planet! See page 30 to figure out which one.

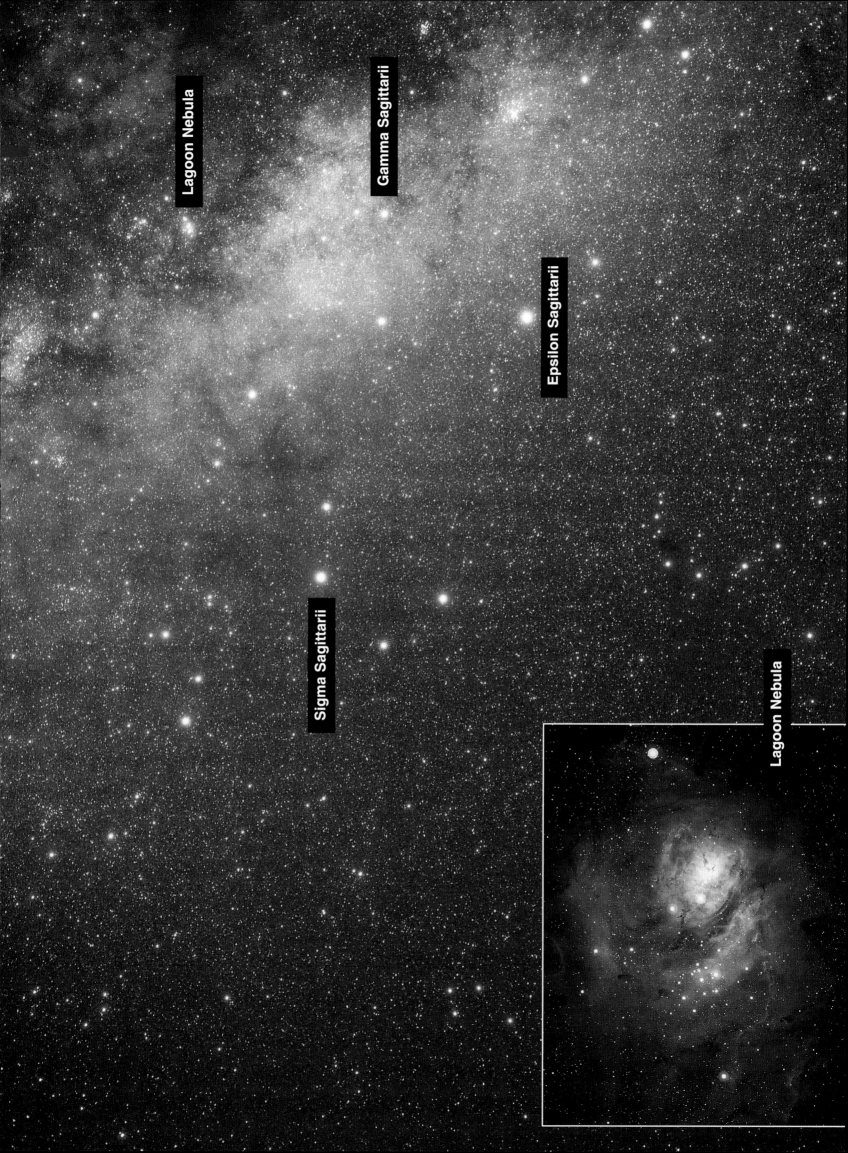

Lagoon Nebula

Gamma Sagittarii

Epsilon Sagittarii

Sigma Sagittarii

Lagoon Nebula

September CASSIOPEIA THE QUEEN

Tonight you can see a constellation that looks like a letter of the alphabet—and a star that may possibly support intelligent life.

In mythology, this constellation, Cassiopeia, was a queen who boasted that she was more beautiful than the sea nymphs, lovely creatures who lived in the sea. The sea nymphs didn't like that. Neither did Neptune, who ruled the sea. He demanded that Cassiopeia's daughter, Andromeda, be chained near the shore, and he sent a sea monster there. But right before the sea monster came, a hero named Perseus (OCTOBER) rescued Andromeda.

As a constellation, Cassiopeia certainly has a lot to brag about. It has five bright stars that are easy to see. The pattern doesn't look like a queen, though. Instead, the stars form the letter M or W. One end is brighter than the other. The yellow box tells you where and when to look. If Cassiopeia is in the northeast, the bright end will be higher than the faint end, as in the photograph. If Cassiopeia is in the northwest, the faint end will be higher, so turn the photograph upside down.

In case you were wondering: yes, there is also a king up there, but it's faint. This constellation, Cepheus, looks like a king as much as the constellation Cassiopeia looks like a queen—which is to say, not at all.

Even though the stars of Cassiopeia make a neat pattern, they have nothing to do with one another, because they are different distances away from Earth. Let's start at the bright end and work our way to the faint end: Beta Cassiopeiae is 54 light-years from Earth, Alpha Cassiopeiae is 230 light-years away, Gamma Cassiopeiae (the central star) is 610 light-years away, Delta Cassiopeiae is 100 light-years away, and Epsilon Cassiopeiae is 440 light-years from us. These stars appear together simply because they are in the same direction from us.

Cassiopeia is in the plane of our Galaxy, the Milky Way, whose brightest stars reside in a disk. When we look into this disk, we see lots of stars—a glowing band that the Greeks thought resembled milk. That's why our Galaxy is called the Milky Way. Unfortunately, it's hard to see this glow nowadays, because light pollution from streetlights washes it out. From where I live, I can't see it. But if you can find a place far from a city, the sky should be dark enough on a moonless night to see the Milky Way.

One of the most interesting stars in Cassiopeia, Eta Cassiopeiae, is just 19 light-years from Earth. To find it, start with Alpha Cassiopeiae and move a third of the way toward Gamma Cassiopeiae, the central star in the W shape. Eta Cassiopeiae is fainter than either. It's a yellow star similar to the Sun, so it may possibly have a planet like Earth, with intelligent beings. Perhaps, when you look at this star, someone up there is looking back at *you*, wondering what is going on around our Sun.

Where and When to Look

On these dates	Look	Around this time
January	Overhead	8 p.m.
February	Northwest	8 p.m.
March	Northwest	8 p.m.
April	Northwest	9 p.m.
May	Low North	10 p.m.
June	Low North	10 p.m.
July	Northeast	10 p.m.
August	Northeast	10 p.m.
September	Northeast	9 p.m.
October	Northeast	8 p.m.
November	Overhead	8 p.m.
December	Overhead	8 p.m.

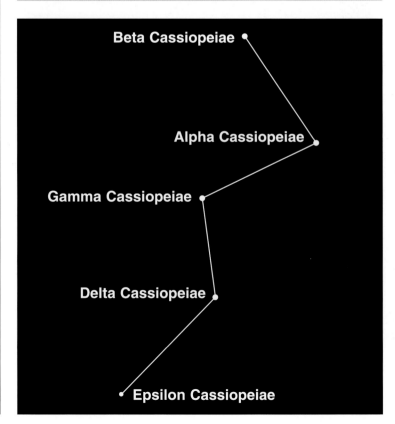

Beta Cassiopeiae
Alpha Cassiopeiae
Gamma Cassiopeiae
Delta Cassiopeiae
Epsilon Cassiopeiae

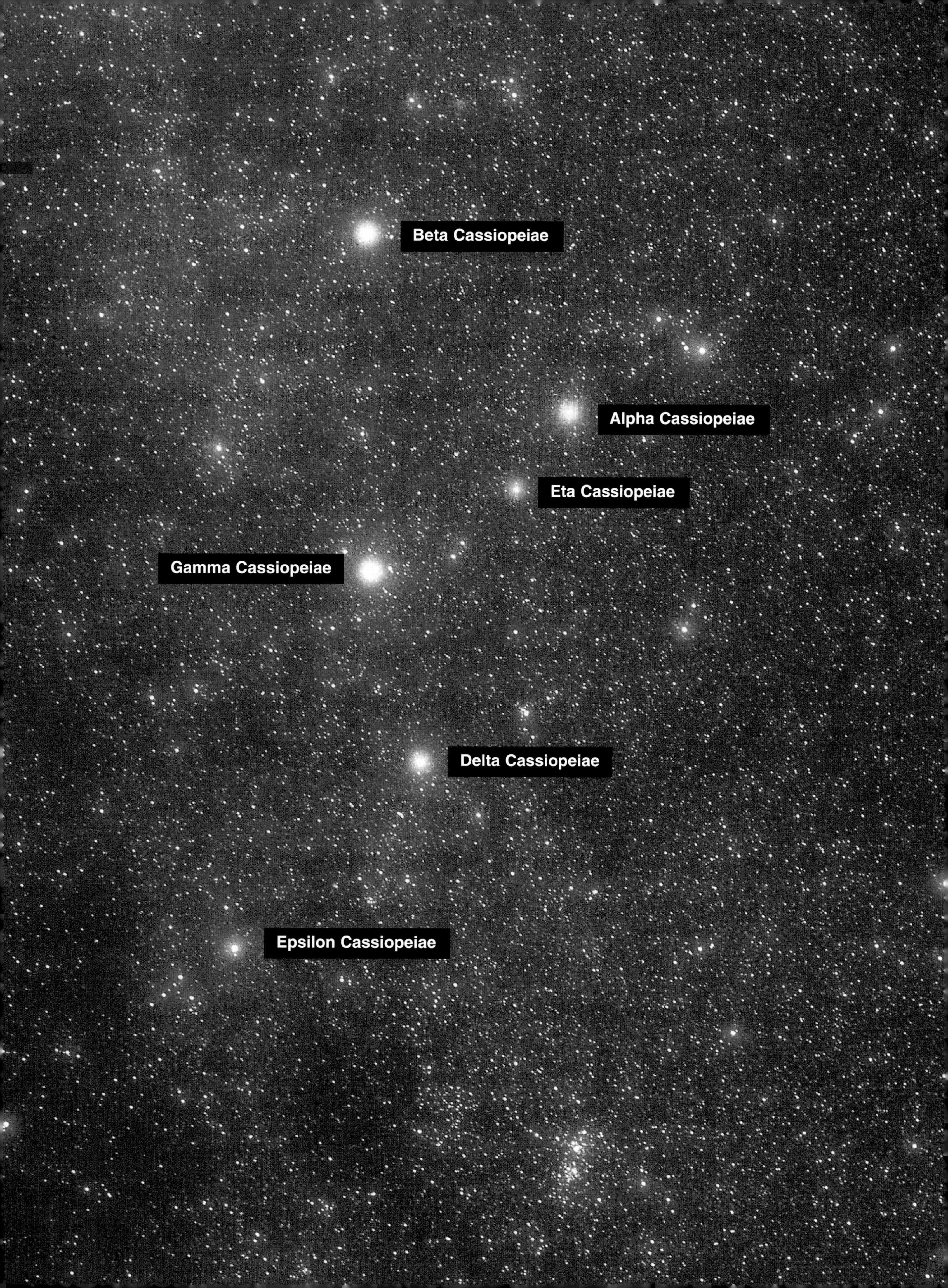
Beta Cassiopeiae
Alpha Cassiopeiae
Eta Cassiopeiae
Gamma Cassiopeiae
Delta Cassiopeiae
Epsilon Cassiopeiae

October
PERSEUS THE HERO

As autumn takes hold, leaves turn red and gold, and nights grow colder and longer. In the sky shines Perseus, bearing a star that will wink at you.

Finding Perseus can be a little tricky, because its stars are not terribly bright, and there are a lot of them. To locate the constellation, look in the direction given in the yellow box and try to find the complicated pattern of stars shown in the diagram. It will probably take you a few minutes.

Perseus possesses a star that astrologers of the Middle Ages thought was dangerous, because the brightness of its light varies. Its name, Algol, even means "the ghoul." Algol's light varies because it has two stars that go around each other. One is brighter than the other. Every 2 days and 21 hours, the fainter star eclipses the brighter one, so Algol fades. Then, a few hours later, the brighter star emerges from behind the fainter one, and Algol brightens.

You can see this without binoculars. Just compare Algol with other stars in Perseus—Mirfak, the constellation's brightest star, and Delta Persei, next to Mirfak, which is fainter. Algol is normally nearly as bright as Mirfak and brighter than Delta Persei. But during an eclipse, Algol looks much fainter than Mirfak and fainter than Delta Persei, too. Try looking at Algol now. What is it doing?

Although Algol is Perseus's most famous star, it is not its brightest. That honor belongs to Mirfak, 600 light-years from Earth, about six times farther than Algol. Mirfak is pale yellow. Look at it through binoculars and you'll see a scattering of other stars. This is Mirfak's star cluster.

Perseus has two other star clusters, which lie side by side, called the Double Cluster. To find the Double Cluster, start with Mirfak, then move to Gamma Persei, then to Eta Persei, and then beyond. If the sky is dark, you may be able to glimpse a hazy patch of light with your unaided eye. But look at it through binoculars and you'll see two dim little glows, right next to each other, sprinkled with many faint stars.

These stars are very far away—7,000 to 8,000 light-years from Earth. That means their light has traveled through space for 7,000 to 8,000 years. The light you are seeing now left those stars when the human race was still in the Stone Age. These stars belong to our Galaxy, the Milky Way, but are so far away that they inhabit a different spiral arm of the Galaxy than we do. If you could view the Milky Way from above, the spiral arms would make it look like a beautiful pinwheel. The Sun and all the other bright stars you see live in what astronomers call the Orion arm. But the Double Cluster resides in the next spiral arm out from the Galaxy's center. Appropriately, it is called the Perseus arm.

Where and When to Look

On these dates	Look	Around this time
October 1 to 15	Northeast	10 p.m.
October 16 to 31	Northeast	9 p.m.
November	East	8 p.m.
December	High East	7 p.m.
January	Overhead	8 p.m.
February	Overhead	7 p.m.
March	West	8 p.m.
April	Northwest	9 p.m.

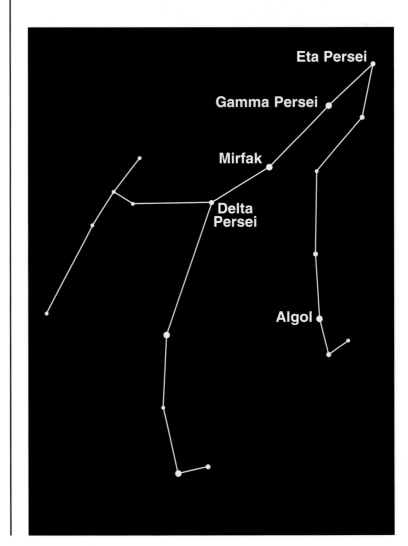

TURN PHOTOGRAPH SO THAT THIS EDGE FACES NORTH.

Double Cluster

Eta Persei

Gamma Persei

Mirfak

Delta Persei

Algol

Double Cluster

November   AURIGA THE CHARIOTEER

A brilliant star shines tonight whose color matches the Sun's.

This star, Capella, leads the constellation Auriga, named for a man who drove a chariot. The constellation itself, though, looks like a pentagon—a five-sided figure. To find it, look in the direction given in the yellow box for one of the brightest stars in the sky. Then try to find the other stars in the pentagon, which are south and east of Capella.

Look at Capella through binoculars. It is golden yellow, the same color as the Sun. It looks much as the Sun would if we saw it from another solar system. A star's color indicates its temperature, so Capella must be as hot as our Sun. Stars that are hotter than the Sun look white or blue, and those cooler than the Sun look orange or red.

However, Capella is not the Sun's twin. Capella is a giant star that sends out about 100 times more light. It is 42 light-years from Earth, yet it looks brilliant. If you viewed the Sun from this distance, you would barely see it.

There's another difference, too. Capella is more than just one star. It consists of two yellow giant stars that go around each other every 104 days— plus two faint red stars, close to each other, which go around the yellow stars every few hundred thousand years. Altogether, then, Capella has four stars, two yellow giants and two red dwarfs, whereas the Sun is just one star. You won't be able to see this through binoculars, though.

Next to Capella is one of the most remarkable stars in the Galaxy, Epsilon Aurigae, which is thousands of light-years from Earth. If you look at it through binoculars, you may say, "What's the big deal?" Well, every 27 years, something huge—perhaps a disk of material—passes in front of the star and blocks some of its light. Normally, star eclipses last just a few hours, but this one lasts *two years.* That's how we know that the eclipsing object, whatever it is, is BIG. Eclipses occur in 2010, 2037, and 2064.

Now let's explore the rest of Auriga. If you like star colors, look at two stars south of Epsilon Aurigae, Eta and Zeta Aurigae. The first is blue, which means it's hotter than the Sun, while the second is orange, which means it's cooler. Use your binoculars to compare their colors.

If you like orange stars, work your way south until you reach Iota Aurigae. Take a look through binoculars at its beautiful orange color. In contrast, the star southeast of it, El Nath, is hot and blue, and the two other stars forming the pentagon— Menkalinan and Theta Aurigae—are white.

Auriga is joined to another constellation, Taurus (DECEMBER). In fact, Auriga's southernmost star, El Nath, officially belongs not to Auriga but to Taurus. So if you can see Auriga, this is probably a good time to track down Taurus.

Where and When to Look

On these dates	Look	Around this time
November 1 to 15	Northeast	9 p.m.
November 16 to 30	Northeast	8 p.m.
December	East	7 p.m.
January	High East	7 p.m.
February	Overhead	8 p.m.
March	High West	8 p.m.
April	West	9 p.m.

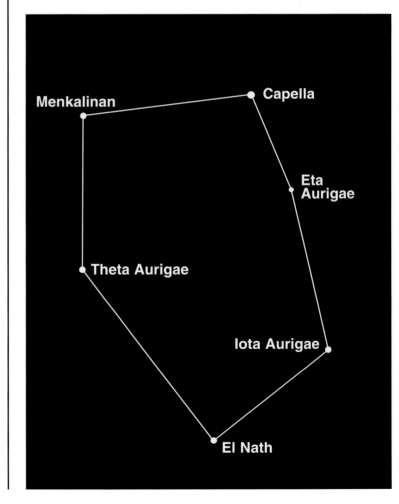

Capella

Menkalinan

Epsilon Aurigae

Eta Aurigae

Zeta Aurigae

Theta Aurigae

Iota Aurigae

El Nath

December
TAURUS THE BULL

December evenings reflect the holidays, with bright stars and colors. In like spirit, Taurus the Bull sports a fiery orange star and the two best star clusters of all.

Part of Taurus looks like the letter V. The five stars at the V's base, including bright Aldebaran, outline the bull's face. Aldebaran is his eye. El Nath and Zeta Tauri are the tips of his horns.

To find Taurus, look in the direction given in the yellow box for a bright, orange star, Aldebaran. Then look for the other stars at the crevice of the V. If you can't find the V, you probably have the wrong star, so try another until you see one that's part of a V. If you know Orion (JANUARY), draw a line from left to right through the belt stars and you'll reach Aldebaran.

Aldebaran is Taurus's brightest star, a sparkling orange giant that sends out 150 times more light than the Sun. It is 65 light-years from Earth and a beautiful sight through binoculars.

Sweep over this region with binoculars and you'll see lots of stars, including the others that make up the V. They belong to the Hyades, the closest star cluster to Earth. These stars are 150 light-years away. They were born together and travel through space together. Believe it or not, Aldebaran does not belong to the Hyades. It is merely a foreground star, not even half as far away as the cluster.

Taurus houses an even better cluster, the incredible Pleiades, which is 400 light-years from Earth. Its brightest stars are blue. The first time I saw the Pleiades, I didn't know it; to my eye, it looked like a tiny cloud. Then I looked at it with binoculars. Wow! I saw dozens and dozens of stars.

You can do the same. If Taurus is in the east, look for the Pleiades above Aldebaran. If Taurus is in the west, look below Aldebaran. As Taurus rises and sets, Aldebaran always follows the Pleiades. In fact, "Aldebaran" means "the follower."

Now check out El Nath, the brighter of the two stars marking the Bull's horn tips. It is blue, 130 light-years away. It doesn't look special, but it marks a special direction: the Galactic anticenter, the point exactly opposite the center of our Galaxy, where we look out to the edge of the Milky Way's disk of stars, some 30,000 light-years beyond El Nath.

Looking toward the edge is good for stargazing. Here's why. Our Galaxy is a spiral. This means that if you saw it from the outside, it would look like a pinwheel, with beautiful spiral arms wrapped around its center. The spiral arms contain the very brightest stars. We live near the inner edge of one spiral arm, the Orion arm. In summer, we look toward the Galactic center, in Sagittarius (AUGUST). But when we look *away* from the Galactic center, as we do in winter, we look into the Orion arm—and the sky is full of spectacle.

Where and When to Look

On these dates	Look	Around this time
November 1 to 15	East	9 p.m.
November 16 to 30	East	8 p.m.
December	East	7 p.m.
January	High East	7 p.m.
February	Overhead	8 p.m.
March	High West	8 p.m.
April	West	9 p.m.

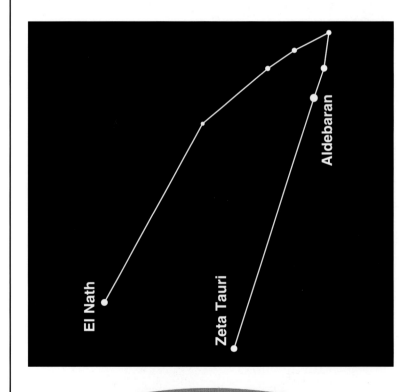

Planet Alert!
If you see a bright "star" in this constellation which is not on the photograph, it is probably a planet! See page 30 to figure out which one.

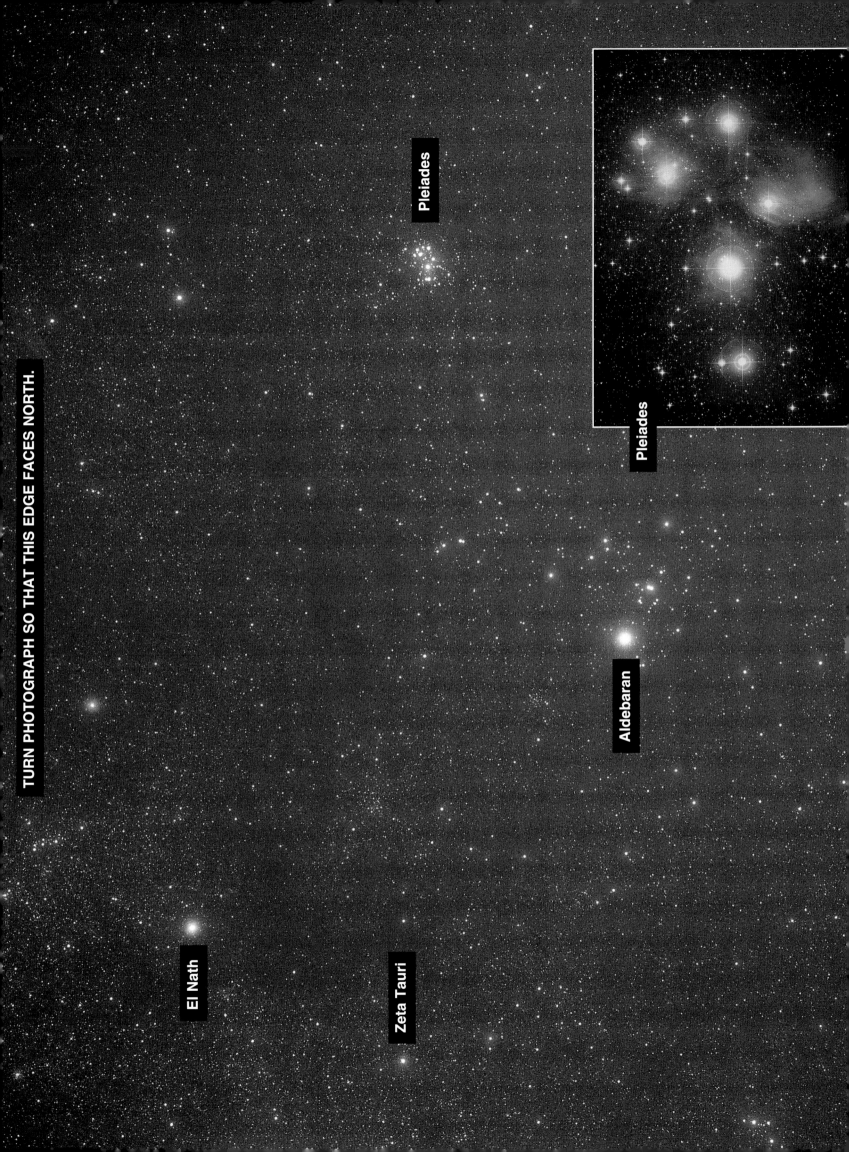

TURN PHOTOGRAPH SO THAT THIS EDGE FACES NORTH.

Pleiades

Pleiades

Aldebaran

El Nath

Zeta Tauri

Planets

We live on a planet, the Earth, that goes around a star, the Sun. The Sun has nine planets: Mercury, Venus, Earth, Mars, Jupiter, Saturn, Uranus, Neptune, and Pluto. Stars make their own light; planets don't, but you can still see planets because they reflect the Sun's light. They merely *look* like stars.

Four planets besides Earth are easy to see: VENUS, MARS, JUPITER, and SATURN. There's a problem, though. Over the months and years, as the planets go around the Sun, they move from constellation to constellation. Fortunately, they do stay near a zone of the sky called the zodiac. Four zodiac constellations are in this book: Leo (MARCH), Scorpius (JULY), Sagittarius (AUGUST), and Taurus (DECEMBER). In these constellations, do you see a bright "star" that's not on the photograph? Congratulations! You've just discovered, or rediscovered, a planet. Now you can try to figure out which one it is:

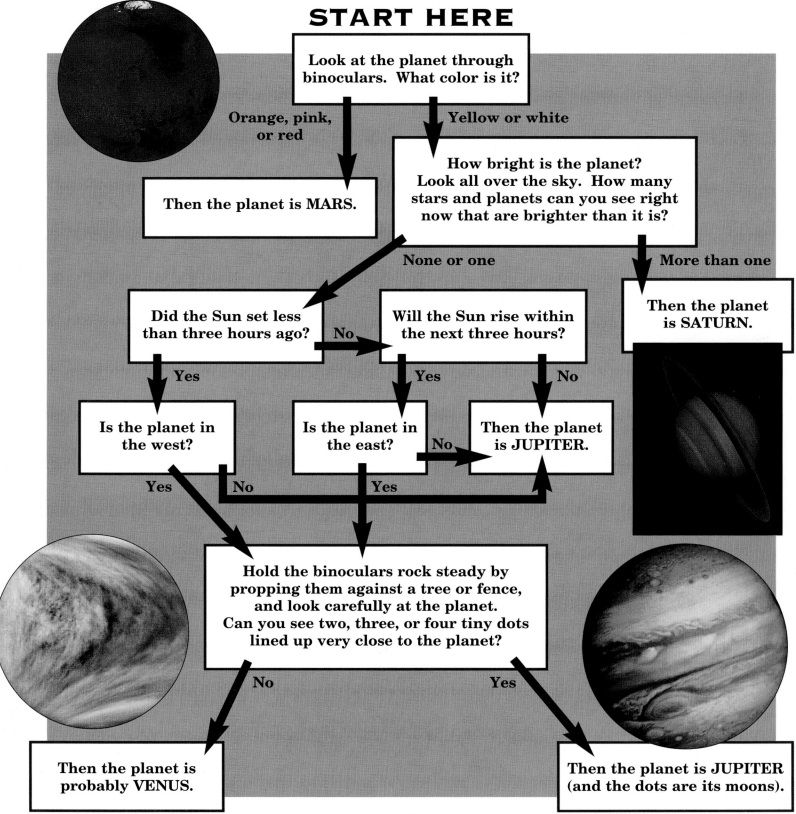

START HERE

Look at the planet through binoculars. What color is it?

Orange, pink, or red → Then the planet is MARS.

Yellow or white → How bright is the planet? Look all over the sky. How many stars and planets can you see right now that are brighter than it is?

None or one

More than one → Then the planet is SATURN.

Did the Sun set less than three hours ago? — No → Will the Sun rise within the next three hours?

Yes → Is the planet in the west?

Yes → Is the planet in the east? — No → Then the planet is JUPITER.

No → Then the planet is JUPITER.

Hold the binoculars rock steady by propping them against a tree or fence, and look carefully at the planet. Can you see two, three, or four tiny dots lined up very close to the planet?

No → Then the planet is probably VENUS.

Yes → Then the planet is JUPITER (and the dots are its moons).

The Brightest Stars

Rank	Star	Constellation	Distance (light-years*)	Color	Page
0	**Sun**	——	0	Yellow	——
1	**Sirius** (SEER-ee-iss)	**Canis Major** (KAY-niss MAY-jur)	8.6	White	January
2	**Canopus** (kuh-NOH-puss)	**Carina** (kuh-REE-nuh)	310	Yellow-white	**
3	**Alpha Centauri** (AL-fuh sen-TORE-ee)	**Centaurus** (sen-TORE-uss)	4.4	Yellow	**
4	**Arcturus** (ark-TOOR-uss)	**Boötes** (boh-OH-teez)	37	Orange	April
5	**Vega** (VAY-guh)	**Lyra** (LIE-ruh)	25	White	May
6	**Capella** (kuh-PELL-uh)	**Auriga** (oh-RYE-guh)	42	Yellow	November
7	**Rigel** (RYE-jull)	**Orion** (oh-RYE-in)	800	Blue	January
8	**Procyon** (PROH-see-on)	**Canis Minor** (KAY-niss MY-nur)	11.4	Yellow-white	——
9	**Achernar** (AY-ker-nar)	**Eridanus** (AIR-ih-DAIN-uss)	144	Blue	**
9	**Betelgeuse** (BEE-tul-JOOZ)	**Orion** (oh-RYE-in)	430	Red	January
11	**Beta Centauri** (BAY-tuh sen-TORE-ee)	**Centaurus** (sen-TORE-uss)	530	Blue	**
12	**Altair** (al-TAIR)	**Aquila** (uh-KWILL-uh)	16.8	White	May
13	**Alpha Crucis** (AL-fuh CREW-siss)	**Crux** (KRUKS)	320	Blue	**
14	**Aldebaran** (al-DEB-er-in)	**Taurus** (TORE-uss)	65	Orange	December
15	**Spica** (SPY-kuh)	**Virgo** (VER-goh)	260	Blue	April
16	**Antares** (an-TAIR-eez)	**Scorpius** (SCORE-pee-iss)	600	Red	July
17	**Pollux** (PAW-lux)	**Gemini** (JEM-ih-nye)	34	Orange	——
18	**Fomalhaut** (FOE-muh-LOE)	**Piscis Austrinus** (PIE-siss awss-TRINE-uss)	25	White	——
19	**Deneb** (DEH-neb)	**Cygnus** (SIG-nuss)	1,800	White	June
19	**Beta Crucis** (BAY-tuh CREW-siss)	**Crux** (KRUKS)	350	Blue	**
21	**Regulus** (REG-yoo-luss)	**Leo** (LEE-oh)	77	Blue	March
22	**Adhara** (add-HARR-uh)	**Canis Major** (KAY-niss MAY-jur)	430	Blue	——
23	**Castor** (KASS-ter)	**Gemini** (JEM-ih-nye)	52	White	——
24	**Gamma Crucis** (GA-muh CREW-siss)	**Crux** (KRUKS)	88	Red	**
25	**Shaula** (SHAW-luh)	**Scorpius** (SCORE-pee-iss)	700	Blue	July

*One light-year is the distance light travels in one year, 5.9 trillion miles, or 9.5 trillion kilometers.

**This star is too far south to see from most northern latitudes.

Index

Individual stars are *italicized*; individual constellations and star patterns are **bold**.